TAKING STOCK

Taking Stock

Miriam N. Kotzin

TAKING STOCK

Copyright © 2011

by Miriam N. Kotzin

Cover art and design: Peter Groesbeck

All rights reserved. No part of this book may be used or reproduced in any manner whatsoever without written permission from the publisher, except in the case of brief quotations embodied in articles and reviews.

Published by

~Star Cloud Press®~
6137 East Mescal Street
Scottsdale, Arizona 85254-5418

ISBN: 978-1-932842-65-4 — $ 12.95

www.starcloudpress.com

Printed in the United States of America

Table of Contents

Backing Sheet	1
Tracks	2
Sunday Photographer	3
Only a Lady Poet	4
Hang Glider	6
The fishwife	7
Resting Place	8
The Foyer	9
The Committed	10
Second Glance	11
Arachne Dances for the Man Who Loves Spiders	12
2 Train	13
E Train	14
Homecoming	15
Mirror Images	16
Self-Portrait	18
Hate Poem	19
Oasis	20
The Web	21
Taking Stock	23
Taxis	25
Warm Rain	27
The Deaf Psychotherapist	28
Dental Work	32
The Callers	33
Adumbration	35
River Swimmer	36
Training	38
Checkout Line	39
Pyromania	41
Script: "Without You"	42

Being Packed	43
Collection	45
Simile	47
Lip Reading	48
Oranges	49
Hair	50
Sunfield	51
Sea Changes	53
Working Late	55
Weather Report	57
Sign Language	58
Floraphilia	59
Cycle	60
Kashrut	61
Close the Door Softly on Your Way Out, Clark Kent	62
Tuscan Journey	64
Fucking Love: A Poem	65
Our Love is Domed	67
not all	68
Man of my Dreams	69
Flat Earth	70
Batwoman at the Cocktail Party	71
Wind	72
Magic Act	73
Machine	75
New	76
Crystal Dinner Bell	77
Renting	78
Blue	80
Punctuation	81
Goshen	82

To Joseph Danciger

Backing Sheet

        All good typing manuals stress the importance
        of using a backing sheet to protect the platen.

For the clever historian
with a talent for detection,
it's all here:
all the rough and polished drafts,
all the impressions,
a complete record
with special sensitivity to pauses.
Fragments and sentences overlap
in inaccessible patterns
lovely as expensive wallpaper,
while punctuation litters the page
like illegible Braille.

I am lost in scrutiny,
in attempts to reconstruct meaning
with only the hesitations
and the questions clear.

Tracks

Words
leave tracks
on the page
as they do
through
our lives,
as small
animals
leave tracks
in the snow

when our
attention
wanders,
erasures-
a body
dragged
by its heels.

Miriam N. Kotzin

Sunday Photographer

Anthurium obvious,
and iris, lupine, calla
lilies: cheap thrills, dangerous
rarely. With this lens, voilà!

Peonies lost innocence,
as did I, caught up, kneeling
before flowers, reticence
gone, voyeuristic wingding.

I saw in a different
way through a lens, and roses
unfolded their insolent
petals, held obscene poses,

but now I watch cyclamen
strain upward. I peer into
camellias. What gentlemen
behave this badly, undo

the past's restraints? Delicious,
my bawdy vision delights
me. I savor lubricious
moments like these sweet insights.

Only a Lady Poet

would write about
asparagus,
thumb-thick, thrusting
almost visibly up
through yielding earth.

Reader, you have
a dirty mind.
I simply meant
a growing crop,
each stalk rising
from a tangle of roots.

Or bunched,
bundled, bound
by a rubber band,
trimmed and loosed
into a pan, simmering.

Most are erect,
but some condescend,
incline their heads
towards others, as at any
cocktail party.

Miriam N. Kotzin

No gentleman poet
would write about
asparagus; gentlemen
poets grow visibly
famous writing
about, say, plums.

Hang Glider

Launched, strapped to the kite
above me, I am carried from the cliff
over a pasture where trees
hold up branches sharp as stakes.
I never thought to soar. I am content
to be carried by currents over earth
that rushes to meet me.

Miriam N. Kotzin

The fishwife

continues her familiar harangue,
shameless through the streets.

I catch sight of myself
in a shop window.
The fishwife continues to rave.
Even in this distorted reflection
my agitation is obvious.

I do not choose to stare her down.
Nothing good can come from looking
a madwoman in the face.

TAKING STOCK

> Resting Place

I know something is wrong
when I lie naked on the bathroom floor,
my body, on the cold squares of tile,
the fuzzy rug, soft and warm, under my ankle,
the sweating bowl, cold against my calf.

I lie here remembering
how in the November rain
the steam grate was comforting as cocoa.
I resisted temptation to face
a room empty of answers, empty
of questions. Speculate how the grate
lured, dangerous as Charybdis,
Scylla, and all the sirens.
What options are left after even
an hour on the grate? On such a busy
street my sister, my twin, was certain
to see me curled, ignoring the rain,
the quick-heeled shoes.

I feel the squares of tiles pressing
my flesh sporty with its new plaid.
I might be a tout in this outfit.
Consider: is this grounds
for dismissal?

Miriam N. Kotzin

The Foyer

When I open the door
for my lover,
a body, dressed
in my black jacket,
falls into the foyer.
The face, as always,
is unrecognizable.
My lover, my twin,
jokes. The body
lies on the floor
between us.

Taking Stock

The Committed

All the best people
have been here:
poets, painters, statesmen;
the man from the next block;
the menopausal woman
who came in for electroshock
and returned home
to her own closet
to hang on a hook.

All have gone down
deep into themselves
and returned
whimpering, gagging, howling
at the slime and stink
of their own gut.

Look over there on the floor:
arms locked around his knees
a man sits rocking,
practicing a silent lullaby.
Listen. Listen.
I live here too.

Miriam N. Kotzin

Second Glance

Look again. I was never
photogenic, but anyone
who saw the picture
flashed on the local news
or buried
in the second section
of the paper would be
disappointed with the likeness.

This last joins the photos
taken through the years
of me, smiling, eyes closed,
standing beside a series
of irrelevant men.
Now I only seem
to blink at life.

I cannot be held
responsible
for the failures
of these photographers,
for my lack of expression.
It may be up to you
to identify the body.
Look again.

Arachne Dances for the Man Who Loves Spiders

I, Arachne, have a use for venom,
but I can kill in other ways,
weaving webs so beautiful
that no man who loves
spiders can destroy them.

I spin for *Bombyx mori*,
the silkworm, who spins her
own coffin.   Think of Arachne
when you hurtle through dark tunnels
of subways and catch the flash
of a window shattered like a web.
In the center is the record of danger.
In the center of the shattering
is the blasted record of Arachne.

I, Arachne, who spun against wisdom,
paid. Grotesque now, spinning,
I dance only for the man who loves
spiders, weave only for him now.
I hang suspended, my work
destroyed, my death withheld.

Miriam N. Kotzin

2 Train

The walls are bleeding
names. One runs over
the next. Only sha-man
is protected by his own
powerful magic.

Lunes a viernes
a cleancut young man
smiles down at us,
Víctimas in two languages.
We are promised relief
from pain, offered
the security of home,
the pleasures of sex,
wealth, *mas café*,
knowledge of the future
until this offer is withdrawn—
no one is safe.

Taking Stock

E Train

> "Do not pass between cars
> while train is in motion."

We hurtle through darkness.
The broken door slams back

in its track. The tunnel air
enters the car, an uneasy spirit.

The lights flicker. I stare at signs,
faces, fading stains on the floor.

I slip off my shoes, leave my purse
on the seat and move to the door.

I straddle the gap between cars, stand with
my hands raised, cold metal under bare feet.

The train twists my body, opens
me wider. Wheels scream.

I am a living X for a moment
of perfect balance on this last ride.

Miriam N. Kotzin

Homecoming

The eclipse of wide fields,
the slow stain of evening,
the sky heavy with birds. . .
I no longer remember
why I chose to walk
naked through the tall rows
of ripening corn.
The blades slit my flesh
to wet red mouths.

Mirror Images

1.
The first man who called me unfeminine
taught Swift, read aloud about the
Brobdingnagian women and their dugs.
"Where's your mirror?" he asked,
and, when I had none, called me
unwomanly. All women carry mirrors.

2.
I have mirrors: boxes of them in the bottom
of my closet; tiny mirrors; mirrors to keep;
mirrors to give away; mirrors my mother gave me
to carry with me so I might always be feminine.

3.
My sentences are my looking glass;
my mirrors are my sentence.
They are prisons defining the length of my sentence;
yet in my silences and yours what confinement.

4.
In these lines I find reflections of myself.
The mirror fogs when you breathe on me.

5.
When you look over my shoulder,
the image in my mirror changes.

6.
If I place the mirror just so between us,
we can see one another, but not ourselves.
It depends on the angle of incidence.

7.
If you stand directly in front of my mirror,
look into it closely, you can see your reflection
by looking through me.

8.
The woman my husband loves
has a voice so soft I cannot hear it.
Yet she is free with my mirrors.
He says she cries out in her sleep

Self-Portrait

Mirrors are everywhere
in my poems,
reflecting in crazy angles
images of myself
and of you, too,
my twin, my sister.

Hate Poem

I know who you are,
Mouse. Your eyes
are like bird droppings.
Your ex-husband
laughs at you with
all your old friends.
You have no friends.
Your tail is twitching.
You eat razor blades
for breakfast.
I will know it
when you die.
Reread this poem.

Oasis

And I thought: your hair
is a tent for your body.
I heard the hot winds
across the desert.
I felt the hot winds.
I felt the sting of the sand.
And I thought of your hair
like a tent.

And I thought: your hair
is a tent for your body.
I saw the silhouettes of raiders
riding dark on the horizon,
their cries lost in the wind.
And I thought of your body
in the tent.

And I thought: your hair
is a tent for your body.
I heard the song
the wind makes
when palms are together.
I thought of clear water.
Your eyes are rain to me now
as I think of your hair (a tent)
and your body.

Miriam N. Kotzin

The Web

Even in January she goes bare-armed,
her hands heavy with silver
spiders and snakes and hollow-eyed skulls,
her wrists weighted and bound
by leather and chains.
On her throat under chains,
a pale scar gleams the width
of discreet surgery, of a slim blade.

She is barefaced and trembles.
And the fine bones of her face
are contradictions.

And even in January she goes bare-armed,
her arms untracked,
but her wrists,
what of her pale wrists?
Under the chains and the leather
do pink lines map the path
of an old flight?

And even in January she goes bare-armed,
on her left shoulder tattooed a blue web,
darker than veins,
a fat red spider,
brighter than blood.

TAKING STOCK

The web spreads wider than my palm,
wider than my fingers can stretch.
I examine my palm, the lines webbed.
I sort out old scars.
I read the lines.
I listen to an octave
beyond my reach.

Miriam N. Kotzin

Taking Stock

When I have fears
that I may cease to be
in Lord and Taylor's basement,
not by bare bodkin
but by knife of stainless
steel and natural wood handle,
I take stock, stroking the blade,
checking for smoothness,
hefting the knife, lifting
it from its box especially
designed for gifting purposes,
despair at cheap goods so done up.
I see the wrist, not neatly slit,
but meaty as a severed hand,
bone, sinews and cartilage;
imagine bleeding on the fawn
rug near the imported Italian pottery,
and being dragged out of danger
by the saleswoman, trying her best
to make me buy a shirt,
assuring me that the price
is right, smiling bully.
I want to scream, scandalous.
Instead I take myself
in hand and up the elevator
to lingerie and loungewear;

TAKING STOCK

I finger the figured silk,
and wonder, keeping silent,
for how long I need to wire
my jaw shut.

Miriam N. Kotzin

Taxis

The responsive movement of an organism toward or away
from an external stimulus.
    American Heritage Dictionary

Because nothing has changed I run out
into traffic, like other women hailing taxis.
Because nothing has changed I stare into
the rearview mirror, like other women riding in taxis.
Because nothing has changed I call out
in my sleep, like other women hailing taxis.
Because nothing has changed I curl into
a corner, like other women riding in taxis.
Because nothing has changed I run out
of excuses, like other women hailing taxis.
Because nothing has changed I change into
a new woman, like other women riding in taxis.
Because nothing has changed I hold out
false hope like other women hailing taxis.

Because nothing has changed I wear
mirrored sunglasses.
Nothing has changed because I wear
mirrored sunglasses.
Because nothing has changed you can
still see yourself.
Because nothing has changed you can

Taking Stock

    still see yourself in my eyes.
You can see yourself in my eyes
because nothing has changed
because nothing has changed
because I wear mirrored sunglasses
you can still see yourself in my eyes.
Because nothing has changed, I fall out
of love, like other women riding in taxis.

Worm Rain

All night the rain poured my dreams.
The gutters were wild with water
and freshets fell into storm drains.
So we woke into the morning
of the worm rain.

The earth is sodden with the long warm rain
that covers the pavements with worms.
At every step a slaughter
of pink and brown wriggling.
Some, half-crushed, survive for a time
stuck to the cement; while others, whole, move
in blind and silent undulations.

The Deaf Psychotherapist

Nothing in his training
had prepared him for this.
At first he merely thought
his cases had become
more interesting.
The stodgy Mrs. Green
murmured she was late
because she had to wait
until her bail
had been posted.
Mr. Brown complained
of fear of ice,
something he'd never
suffered from before.
"If it's unbearable,
until you're cured
winter in Miami,"
said the therapist.
Mr. Brown, whose proudest moment
was winning a contest
for the child having the most
freckles, frowned.
Mrs. Green, who, past fifty,
sewed ruffles on all her clothes,
was agitated.
"Not a banana," she said.
"Not a banana at all."

Miriam N. Kotzin

He decided to listen
only to the tones
and the rhythms.
He listened
to his patients'
music.

He hoped someday to hear
one of Beethoven's late quartets;
this was the dream
of every psychotherapist.
Mrs. Green, however,
was locked
in an eternal foxtrot.
Mr. Brown was a series
of Strauss waltzes.
This was an agony,
yet he persisted.

One day, a balding popeyed gnome
waddled into the office.
When the little man
opened his mouth,
it was Schubert's "Trout."
"You don't need me,"
cried the psychotherapist.
"We should all be so healthy,"
he added-
although he could not help staring
at the Alpine hat and lederhosen

of this lucky fellow.
"I cannot hear you,"
mourned the gnome.
"I am here because
whenever anyone speaks to me,
I hear no words,
only music."

The psychotherapist had never
learned to read minds.
Now he thought momentarily
of learning to read lips,
learning-why not-
to read whole bodies.
He developed a revolutionary
new method of treatment.
He planned a series of articles
for *The New England Journal of Medicine*.

Whatever expressions
his patients wore,
whatever movements they made,
however slight,
these he himself adopted.
By assuming their expressions,
their positions,
he understood them
perfectly.
In turn they responded
with the next and the next

thought and movement.
He practiced his mime.
A slight exaggeration.
He and his patients moved
around the office
like unsynchronized shadows.
He began to wear whiteface,
to paint on a bright red mouth
and dark arched brows.
He wore a black leotard
and blue overalls
and a black and white striped
tee-shirt for his sessions.

Each day it took him longer
to put on his make up.
He became lonely in the office;
one after another
his patients stopped coming
without his ever having heard
even one
of Beethoven's late quartets
from any of them.

At last he recognized
the truth. "I have rid
the world of madness.
I must become a potter
or a surgeon."

He sat alone with his thoughts,
a mime without gesture.

Dental Work

Even the best intentioned
hands can slip.
I wait for the cheap thrill
of short-lived pain.
Agape and drooling,
still I would be affable.
When asked, I spit, open
wider, turn my head a bit;
in short, I cooperate.
Now it's hopeless
to aspire to wit, to join
the jesting that passes
over my head,
that is meant to amuse
me, the patient. Bibbed
and trapped, I would
seem effortlessly brave.

Hours later, the numbness
is gone. From such experiences,
synapses activate. New
metal and old arc:
through galvanic reactions,
I gain a new sense of myself.

Miriam N. Kotzin

The Callers

I.
I couldn't place the voice
he knew my secret name
the color of my room
the pattern on the walls
he knew everything
and he promised
my parents gone from the house
he knew I was alone
and the windows open
the summer heat
and the screen doors to catch
whatever breeze
and his voice so soft
with promise
and he said to meet him
at the corner in ten minutes
calling me softly again
and again showing how well
he knew my secret name.

II.
He had been by for my roommate
whose giggles filled the room with suds.
I was clever and silent while he tried
to ferret it out until the night
when I was alone and he called

Taking Stock

to tell me everything
he had known all along
how to call me by name
softly unbuttoning
his voice was the heat and the breeze
I did just what he said.

III.
Night after night his calls
rocked us to terror
he knew what the directory omitted
he told me my husband's secret name
he tried with his laughter
to weave my dreams into new patterns.
He left me his number.
Now I barely remember his voice.
I wrote nothing down.
I do not intend to call him back.

Adumbration

Each day, new lessons, from
a hard master. Too long I've been
dumb and deaf and numb. Now his
fingers, lips, tongue articulate
my body's Braille alchemy. These
secrets, easiest revealed, transmute,
lift and open. I learn to hold my
breath, to breathe, to catch his
breath's rhythm, to match gasps
and clutch with his final shudder.
With patient repetitions he reminds
me, teaches the long slow essential:
not letting go, never having to hold.

River Swimmer

> "A great disorder is an order."
> Stevens

He crushes her hair
in his fist,
wraps it around his hands,
twists it, crushes
until she feels
all the molecules of her body
rearranging themselves
until she has changed irrevocably
become-though not without shame-
Elizabeth Barrett Browning counting.

I fear the sonnet form cannot contain
my feelings, Robert dear. And yet it must.
Tonight I sit and think about those long
and dreary years at home before you wrote
to me. And then your letters filled my life
until you came for me yourself. We stole
away. I never thought to have such strength,
and when strength failed, you took me in your arms
and up the stairs, across the stream-Vaucluse!
How do I love you? Let me count the ways
and find the form.

He kisses her eyelids.
She is afraid to open her eyes,
to see how it looks now.

Elizabeth, what you felt
when Browning unbuttoned your white bodice,
slipped off that linen:
you lay quiet,
trembling as the whiteness fell
from your body and you, darkly waited,
his gaze, his hands moving over your slightness.
The spaniel was banished,
you mastered, inadequacies
vanishing under his direction;
you forgot to worry about your breasts,
your coloring, your hips in his hands
until

        I know how it was
your body a confused landscape of hills
and valleys suddenly ordered, then again
changing as his hands re-created you.

My body becomes a swift river:
you, a strong swimmer;
the river flows with no banks,
swimmer; I, river, current,
am carried by current
towards you, towards, lagging,
towards with again with,
with you, swimmer.

Taking Stock

Training

As in any bad movie
the train whistle mourns.

The train moves through
its own sad hoot.

Sound bridge.

Through bleared windows
the world is half-lost.

All edges soft focus;
fields given over to haze.

Slow dissolve.

The whistle clears the track
of small boys, balancing

on the humming rail as though
they carry buckets of water.

Fade.

Easygoing, you
are at the end of the line,

a long shot.

Miriam N. Kotzin

Checkout Line

I wheel my cart up the aisles and down
again, past soups, paper goods, caustic
cleaners and around to fresh produce
where boys scoop up glistening cherries
and eat them on the spot,
spitting the pits at my feet, making
a game of it.

           That's all right.
I get mine in line, twenty minutes
once a week with the checkout clerk;
I know his body as well as any man's.
Pushing thirty, he's fading fast, but
with eyes I'd pay to drown in.
Hey, fella, wanna be in pictures?

What's missing here is the shock I felt
when I stood by the register and
saw, for the first time, him standing naked;
saw his Apollo's Girdle slightly gone to fat;
saw the minute wrinkles on his torso.
What's missing is my wondering how
to meet his gaze when I had to raise my eyes
after he'd finished breaking the change rolls
and the shower of spilling silver was over.
Of course by now he must be used to

Taking Stock

lines of women and men waiting to take him.
But I stop well short of that:
am satisfied weekly
to watch him stand naked by the register;
to watch the slow progress
of his most beautiful decay.

Pyromania

> "Persons whose lungs are delicate should by no
> means use Lucifers."
> Warning on a box of Lucifer matches, 1829

People who play with matches
learn the smell of sulfur,
seek the quick liquescence
that fuels the flare to flame.
People who play with fire
know the cool cone flickers
at the center of each flame,
find in bright burning bodies
cheap alchemy.

TAKING STOCK

Script: "Without You"

"Jezebel or tease?" I watch his
eyes flick down and back up twice,
attempting my measure. He
neatly takes the lead. At first I'm a
coward: I hesitate, backpedal, but end
laughing. I subtitle my conversation.
Accidentally I spill my words
down the front of my blouse,
excuse the affront of my blush. Fade.

"Brace yourself, sweet,..." We
race through old lyrics, translating
as we go into our private Esperanto,
declining nothing at all. We reinvent a
lingo to explore, to inventory in a format
edited to fit our screen. I play ingénue,
you genuine. We promise to keep in touch.

Miriam N. Kotzin

Being Packed

Crude to ask how many cc. You
say, "Hang on for dear life." I

don't know where you want me
to put my legs, my arms, what

you like me to do when you
make your moves, but I expect

to hear, "Anytime you don't like
it we can stop."

               I rode
crossbar years before you

came along. It took a while
until I got the hang of it,

to lift my legs, bend my torso
back. It was a balancing act

until I learned to move
without thinking, all my

body responding to taking
curves. He'd slow down or

TAKING STOCK

speed up without warning. I
was heedless of danger, knew

only the ride. After all, he
was taking me straight home.

Miriam N. Kotzin

Collection

Crimson
carmine
vermilion
today's trash, plastic bags, in artless
imitation of that sculpture
at the Modern,
basic black bulging chic,
charcoal green shade of the fifties,
and one shocking translucence
in reds and pinks
scarlet cardinal

sins of lipstick stubs
drying in a box of souvenirs:
Persian Melon
Tahitian Sunset
Van Gogh Sunflower
Tangee Natural
all but Luvlee
which we pubescent literalists
crooned Loo-vlee.

Lou, Lou, skip to my Lou
when we could do anything
we wanted to our faces:
eyelids enameled blue, green,

lids lined thick
with thoughts of kohl
and Cleopatra who on her barge floated
down the Nile of our fantasies.

My lips are rarely pale these days.
My body makes its own bloom.

Together we are new.
Unshared memories arrive
unsolicited as a chain letter.
We cannot empty ourselves
like houses of the deceased
cleaned by distant relatives
who bundle everything
to the curb.

Simile

When winter is only a habit of mind
a tree is like a woman at dusk
who has been waiting
all day for her lover
whose arrival is certain.

Or perhaps the woman,
pregnant with desire,
is like a tree, rooted,
whose each graceful motion
in the wind
is incidental.

Like a woman, rooted, like a tree,
unfolding when winter
is only a habit of mind.

Lip Reading

The moon, pale
as wax, fills
the only empty
corner of the sky,
wanton as
sleek white
rain.

By this light
I cannot read
your lips
with my eyes.

Miriam N. Kotzin

Oranges

I have watched you peel
oranges with a spoon, insinuate
the bowl beneath the rind with
practiced moves. I've
been accustomed to knives
and was amazed to see
you peel it clean with spoon
and fingers the first morning I
found you standing at the kitchen
counter, naked, peeling,
pulling apart the sections,
eating, a blue and white plate
heaped with rind.
                              Mornings,
now, the kitchen is fragrant with
oranges and coffee. You come to
find me in the bedroom, dressing, and
hold out a section of orange.
I open my mouth, amazed, ready
for all you offer.

Hair

Each time I tell myself
I will be leaving you
part of myself as
though I want to take you
by surprise, want you
to discover me
again.

      I will never miss
these silver and dark strands
like a scrawled note
held by a magnet on a fridge,
others hidden among
cabbage roses on sofa cushions,
and on the pillowslip where
my hair spills in rivulets
you catch, fisting them,
looking down at my parting lips,
my half-closed eyelids fluttering.
In the morning I am gone.
I tell myself
I will never miss
what I leave behind.

Miriam N. Kotzin

Sunfield

Even in spring the light
is crystalline, the sky polarized.
But for the road we traveled,
well marked to note the deaths
of those who took the curves
too fast or swerved to avoid
what we'll never know,
this mountain pass would seem
unreal. We have come here
to stand at he edge of this field
you'd remembered, offering me
details like bonbons.
We keep our backs to the white
markers, face the field
waist high with white
and gold. At home, we'd know
the name properly: daisy.

The wind shifts, and the air fills
with the scent of the wild field.
Your hand on my shoulder, you lead
me into the field; the foliage
brushes my legs. It's just
as you said; as we walk in,
the flowers take flight.
Our path is marked by a white

Taking Stock

abandon. The air is sunlight
on wings. We stand still,
and the air stills, settles
without darkening. We are
surrounded by green, gold,
the white that will quicken
at our slightest motion. It is
for this we have come
such a long way.

Miriam N. Kotzin

Sea Changes

I stand on rock-bound shore to watch you race
across the open water, across light-
filled space. I watch as you grow small, until
your distant sail at last begins to turn
on the horizon, moving back. In time
I see you wave. I want to hold my breath.

Your boat begins to slow as though no breath
of wind is stirring, yet the white clouds race
across the azure sky. I'm marking time:
I pace along the dock; I wait. The light
is solid here in summer. And I turn
to watch you tack your way to shore until

I feel myself begin to rise, until
my feet no longer touch the dock. My breath
comes quicker as I rise. I watch you turn
to see me float above your mast. You race
to catch the wind before I'm gone. I'm light
at noon, I'm air. You catch the wind in time,

I ride the wilder current out of time.
You fill your sail. I soar, then slow until
we move together, until all's sunlight,
until we're nothing but one long deep breath,
a shuddering in tandem: our hearts race
one against the other. And then we turn

to go on back to land where we two will turn
back to ourselves. Or so I think. This time
we stay on water, we dissolve. We race
together: sea and air, a mist, until
we're disembodied, both, each other's breath
our own. We have become our own sweet light,

all honeyed. Love, my love...I call you light-
ly now, "my love," as, easily, we turn
to one another. Finally, a breath-
less laugh. And we are back once more in time;
in time, again I call you "love" until
I find you--gone. The tattered white clouds race

away. You who were light to me, in time
have turned to nothing bright. I'll wait until
your breath inspires one last long blind race.

Miriam N. Kotzin

Working Late

Drifting towards sleep,
I listen for clusters of clicks,
clattering a record
of your neurons firing while
you work out problems.
You are in the other room,
staring, your fingers
poised over the keys
as though ready to coax
some new melody to life, not
formula but discovery.
Significant difference.
Define operationally.
The numbers disappear,
and the screen fills with
sunfields of white and yellow,
terraced hillsides, sun-
warmed rocks, water. Sudden
probabilities school like
fish, tropically fluorescent,
turning.
        I listen for sounds
that can mean "save," "save as,"
"replace existing," "cancel."
The final "save." Until
at last you lie here

Taking Stock

with me where together
we travel, tacking, our
sail like a wing, perfect,
filling with sunlit wind.

Weather Report

I can tell you the weather
in all fifty states
isobar by isotherm.

I will tell you about the weather
long distance.
Whisper in your ear
how the drought continues
in Albuquerque.   How in
1816 it snowed in July.

How the record high of the day
took place in 1903, the low
in 1953.   How last night
the report of the record rainfall
for the month was uninterrupted
by any expression of emotion
including yours.

Sign Language

The Kiowa sign,
hands brought together,
thumbs tucked under,
index fingers extended-
"I love you."
One hand moves
across the belly.
"I am hungry."
Hands together.
"I love you."
How to say,
"I am hungry, love,
for you."

Some words
still come hard to me.
Once said, they are smooth
as river stones.

Floraphilia

The amaryllis
pushes its thick head up
in slow rise
straight.
I thought
it would take
forever
until it flowered
(who would suspect)
into me
a blasphemy of scarlet
handspans scarlet
scarlet
until it darkened
like blood
like an essential light
extinguished.

Cycle

Waiting for the bleeding
to begin again,
waiting for the first sign of blood,
checking mornings
for a small spot in the hollow
of my diaphragm
like blood in an egg

you want to leave nothing
of yourself within me.
It's only a matter of time
for the first signs,
for the blood.

Kashrut

The shell's mottled white.
You'll crack it open
only to find blood
in this poem.

Observant,
you can't excise the stain.
You try;
bleeding begins again.
You'll discard this poem
unclean.

Close the Door Softly on Your Way Out, Clark Kent

I could see he was nervous
without his glasses
as he loosened his tie,
unbuttoned his shirt.

His chest was bright blue.
Always polite,
I pretended not to notice.
Even the red and yellow emblem,
the giant S,
I, always a lady, ignored.
Then he unzipped his trousers,
slipped off his shorts.
Still he appeared dressed.
The belt, the costume,
was perfect trompe l'oeil,
even the folds of the cape.
The tattoo artist
had, of course,
taken certain liberties,
made certain painful,
touchy decisions.
It was worth it.

Miriam N. Kotzin

When he left in the morning
dressed in his tweeds,
the doorman didn't look twice.

But my friends knew
by my face
something strange and wonderful
had happened.
They asked all
the obvious questions.
In my modesty,
I declined to answer.

Tuscan Journey

We had left the red-roofed villa far below,
and, back to the sun, you set your foot on a rock.

The fabled wine, air, hills had become merely wine, air, hills.
Cypress shadows fell across the winding road.

While you speak, I keep my eyes fixed on a large black bird
as she spirals so high she cannot hear your voice.

Miriam N. Kotzin

Fucking Love: A Poem

He wants me wide open-
open-hearted, spread wide, open-
mouthed for him, he wants
another devotional.
But he doesn't know
that the other night when I
went to light the gardenia-
scented candle, I opened
a matchbook on his bureau
and found scrawled in violet
ink some Teri's name and number
(that's Teri with an i).
And the next morning
when I looked the matchbook
was gone from his bureau,
and he doesn't smoke
unless he's been smoking with
Teri (with an i) or
other women whose names
end in terminally cute vowels.
And one night his hair
freshly washed, supposedly at
the gym, smelled like some
tropical flower Body Works shampoo
no guy would be caught
dead buying. I kept quiet.

Taking Stock

I've kept on humming.
I've been acting lovey-dovey,
all mooney, Juney, crooney tuney,
but for him now there's going to be
no fucking love poem.

Miriam N. Kotzin

Our Love is Domed

Our love is domed
like the sky
blew through our
lives like a gust
ripped branches
from trees
like a breeze
barely stirred
leaves. Our
love is domed [sic].

TAKING STOCK

    not all

 poems
   rhyme

 you, for
 instance

Miriam N. Kotzin

Man of my Dreams

My lover is taller,
and younger, and happier
with his new girlfriend
than he ever was with me.
He is quick to tell me so.

He describes a practice,
something like suttee,
involving beautiful women.
It guarantees happiness
for their lovers.

His bed is littered
with charred effigies.
He tells me again
how happy he is.
He smiles his wonderful smile.
He strikes a match.
He says I am still beautiful.

I escape with my life.

Flat Earth

Your eyes map the night.
Leaving, you left
a darkness I cannot compass.
Within me, mutinies ride wild
in the night; chartless,
seeking new routes, I sail,
relentless, to the edge.

Miriam N. Kotzin

Batwoman at the Cocktail Party

Like wings my dark wishes enfold me.
I hang here upside down,
unnoticed, contained as a package.
But what if I were to unfurl
my black crepe wings and flit,
unsteady as the inebriate guest?

Across the room stand my old
lover and his new mistress
whom I have been watching
all evening. If I were to circle,
to kiss them with my wings, she
would say only, "How droll,"
and he would say nothing at all.

Taking Stock

Wind

When the wind was right,
Hamlet knew hawk from handsaw.
Our madness knows no compass.
Choose hurricane blasts.
There is more in silence
than the wind blows:
indifference, before which
even reeds must break.

Miriam N. Kotzin

Magic Act

With care I write your name
out of my life into my past
where like other memories
you will languish, in a slow
vanishing act, a neat trick.
I write this sentence
as though with a few
strokes I might banish
you from the present tense
with possibilities.
                Once, love,
you were not an abstract
noun; you were a wild cyclist
urging me to ride; you were
a dancer whose moves made
me dizzy, you were a sleeper
whose dreams summoned me.
When I entered your world
we stirred a field of flowers
into life as startled white
butterflies took flight. I
was air, I was sunlight on water;
together we were wind filling
a sail. We were at our best
disembodied.

Taking Stock

            Now I roll a cabinet
onto stage, mirrored sides
flashing in the spotlight.
I fold down the panels,
reassemble the rig. Obliging,
you step inside while everyone
watches. I tap all six sides.
Drumroll, please.
                When I open
the door, you are gone, my
last, my best illusion.

Miriam N. Kotzin

Machine

Wanting to reach you
I phone again and again.
Each time, in the same words
a woman's voice answers me evenly.
You cannot come to the phone.
She urges me not to hang up,
to leave a message.
Wherever I go
I hear her voice
like swift water over stones.
It might be my own.

One night I call so late
we should all be sleeping.
I am surprised when
you answer, your voice taut.
Close by I hear laughter
like struck crystal
like swift water over stones.

New

The kettle whistles in the other room.
Lying in bed, it seems to her as though
the kitchen does not belong to her. Sun-
light falls in parallelograms. Some day
soon she should buy blinds, or maybe curtains.

She can imagine just how the thin plume
of steam wavers. She does not really know
how long the kettle has been whistling. None
of the old framed photos faces her way.
But she's bought a pot of pink cyclamens

to remind her of home. "You can't assume
anything," she says aloud, and in slow
motion rises from her bed; "anyone
would tell you that. Now." She hears music play
through the party wall. Schubert's Trout opens.

Her kettle joins the quintet and her gloom
floats away on the streams. A small rainbow
hangs in the steam over the kettle. "Well, Hon,"
she says to herself, "it's a sign you'll stay.
Safe. No more floods." We make our own omens.

Miriam N. Kotzin

Crystal Dinner Bell

I see myself mirrored
in this crystal bell
standing silent, useless
in an empty house,
only a dust collector,
nothing more. An ornament
of another age.

Taking Stock

Renting

So far no one has thought
to butcher the forsythia that
arcs in a long wild line
and curves around to the lane.
From the kitchen window I
can see the bending branches. A
male cardinal perches high,
his mate some branches below. He
swings in the winter wind.
Although I know they can find
plenty to eat in the woodland
around the house, still I hung
seed bells, food until spring,
hoping to keep the birds close
for company in this rented house.

I've wintered over here once
before and watched. Since
I came, a whole year of bloom,
almost nothing my own. Can you blame
me for doing so little
planting? I had not thought I'd settle
in so long. I found a white drift
of snowdrops, then daffodils and a blue raft
of grape hyacinths. In late May
twenty peonies, enough for me to cry

over when I'm gone. The terraced
garden's fine for herbs to harvest.
This year I'll put in thyme, lemon thyme,
oregano, and certainly some
rosemary. I'll plant one rose for
the next woman to find when I am far
from this place. I like to think how
she will watch and wait for the show
of buds, wonder at the gifts of bloom
unknown women left to grace her home.
What is it that I leave behind
when I leave these for her to find?

Blue

Even as you lay sleeping
the sky filled the room.
Your breath was sweet as grass.
Together, we were the perfect
conjunction of all the best stars.

Mornings we laughed at our dreams:
One night the Pathet Lao
sniped from under the living room furniture.
Another night you captured
a perfect clean energy source
at great personal danger
to make the world safe
from the OPEC nations.
And once the pilings
of the Steel Pier were rotting
and the Diving Horse was in danger
of drowning. Oh my hero,
goodnight, goodnight, Mr. Calabash
wherever you are.

Miriam N. Kotzin

Punctuation

Doubtless, you, too, have lain awake nights,
dry eyes fastened on the unseen ceiling.
And, doubtless, you have turned the light
on and off and on again, and sat up
certain that if just one detail were set right,
a dripping faucet silenced, perhaps,
that one detail, once ordered, would order all
and let sleep settle. And, doubtless,
you, too, have slept on half an empty bed,
and doubtless morning came.

Goshen

We lie, warming, adrift,
timeless, on the dock.
I watch the wind trifle
with the water's surface
until I grow dizzy
with senseless movement.
The lake burns in the sun.
A hawk cuts a singular
circumference in the still
afternoon. I am a stranger,
but when the light is perfect
the water, reflecting,
returns the world to itself.
I write this to return.

ACKNOWLEDGMENTS

"Hang Glider," *Open Wide*, issue 11, July 2004; "The Fishwife," *Press 1*, Vol. 1, No. 3, January-April 2008; "The Committed," *Pulpsmith*, Vol. 4, No. 1 (Spring 1984), p. 79; "Second Glance," poem, *Rumble*, August 2004; "Arachne Dances for the Man Who Loves Spiders," *Segue*, November 2004; "Mirror Images," *For Poetry*, April 2004; "Oasis," *Taurus*, No. 11 (November 1983), p.4; "Taking Stock," *Maverick Magazine*, July 4, 2004; "Taxis," *Press 1*, Vol. 1, No. 3, January-April 2008; "Worm Rain," *Blaze: Quarterly Literary Magazine*, April 2004; "The Deaf Psychotherapist," *edifice WRECKED!* July 2004; "Dental Work," *Word Riot*, May 14, 2004; "The Callers," *Poems Niederngasse*, August/ September 2004; "Adumbration," *frigg: a magazine of fiction and poetry*, January 2005; "River Swimmer," *Segue*, November 2004; "Checkout Line," *Painted Bride Quarterly*, No. 48, p.33, and reprinted in *Circle Magazine*, Summer 2004; "Being Packed," *Poems Niederngasse*, erotic supplement, February 2006; "Simile," *Plum Ruby Review*, June/July issue 2004; "Hair," *Thieves Jargon*, October 15, 2004; "Sea Changes," *Three Candles*, March 2004; "Floraphilia," *Twenty1Lashes*, Winter, 2005; "Close the Door Softly on Your Way Out, Clark Kent," *Flashquake*, June 1, 2004; "Fucking Love: a poem," *Thieves Jargon*, September 23, 2004; "Flat Earth" as "Columbus," *Mid-South Review*, April 2005; "Only a Lady Poet," *For Poetry*, April 2004; "Batwoman at the Cocktail Party," *Era*, Vol. 12 (Spring 1977), p.11; "New," *Iron Horse Literary Review*, Vol. 3, No. 1, p. 27; "The Crystal Dinner Bell," *Era*, Vol. 10 (Winter 1973), p.11; "Renting," *Word Riot*, May 14, 2004; "Goshen" and "Oranges" *Small Spiral Notebook*, Spring 2004; " Lip Reading," *Riverbabble*, Issue 16 (Winter 2010); "The Web" and "E Train," *Patapsco Review*, 1 (Fall 2010).

About the Author

MIRIAM N. KOTZIN is Professor of English at Drexel University where she teaches creative writing and literature. She also co-directs Drexel's Certificate Program in Writing and Publishing. *Taking Stock* is her third collection of poems, joining *Reclaiming the Dead* (New American Press, 2008), *Weights & Measures* (Star Cloud Press 2009) and a collection of flash fiction, *Just Desserts* (Star Cloud Press, 2010). She is also the author of *A History of Drexel University* (Drexel University Press, 1983). Her fiction and poetry have been published widely online and in print. Nominated five times for a Pushcart Prize, her poetry has been published in such places as *The Southern Humanities Review, Confrontation, Offcourse, Eclectica* and *Boulevard.* She also writes creative nonfiction. She is a contributing editor of *Boulevard* and a co-founding editor of *Per Contra.*

www.ingramcontent.com/pod-product-compliance
Lightning Source LLC
Chambersburg PA
CBHW030003050426
42451CB00006B/103